the moon was back on America's mind. In January Alan B. Shepard scored the longest moon walk recorded to date, strolling the lunar surface for a total of 9 hours. On July 26, Apollo 15 astronauts changed one small step for man to one short ride, steering the four-wheel-drive lunar dune buggy, "the Moon Rover," through the Sea of Rains.

'71

NEW YORK GOVERNOR NELSON ROCKEFELLER ORDERED STATE TROOPERS TO STORM THE STATE CORRECTIONAL FACILITY IN ATTICA, ENDING A FOUR-DAY PRISONER REBELLION IN WHICH 10 GUARDS AND 32 INMATES LOST THEIR LIVES.

It was the year America began its second decade of involvement in Vietnam. May saw 10,000 anti-war protesters march on Washington. On June 30, the Supreme Court upheld the right of the *New York Times* to publish the Pentagon Papers, which detailed a top secret study of U.S. machinations in Indochina. By November, Richard Nixon had announced the withdrawal of 45,000 troops.

newsreel

Flower Children no longer seemed so flowery as the Manson family was found guilty of first-degree murder in the death of Sharon Tate and 6 others. Charles Manson, Leslie Van Houten, Susan Atkins and Patricia Krenwinkel were all condemned to the gas chamber.

On April 25, East Pakistan declared its independence as Bangladesh. India supported the independent nation and sent troops to help fight the invading West Pakistani army. West Pakistani troops surrendered, and a cease-fire was declared.

international

headlines

In Uganda, Major General **idi amin dada** overthrew the government of President Milton Obote. Leaving a bloodbath in his wake, Amin solidified his control by dissolving Parliament and outlawing political parties.

AUSTRIAN DIPLOMAT KURT WALDHEIM
WAS ELECTED UN SECRETARY GENERAL.

ON AUGUST 2, THE UNITED STATES SAID THAT IT WOULD NOT BLOCK ADMISSION OF THE PEOPLE'S REPUBLIC OF CHINA TO THE UNITED NATIONS.

FLASH!

In Northern Ireland,

brian faulkner

became prime minister. Violence escalated after the new government invoked emergency powers of preventive detention to arrest suspected leaders of the Irish Republican Army.

In the Philippines, a primitive tribe called the Tasaday was discovered in a remote mountain region. The tribe used Stone Age tools, and had no words for "hate" or "war."

EMPEROR HIROHITO OF JAPAN WAS GREETED IN ANCHORAGE, ALASKA, BY PRESIDENT NIXON. HIROHITO WAS THE FIRST EMPEROR IN JAPANESE HISTORY TO JOURNEY ABROAD.

DISNEY WORLD opened in Florida.

In a radical departure from military tradition, the U.S. Army changed its bayonet drill shout from **"kill! kill!"** to **"yah! yah!"**

shopping spree

TERRYCLOTH ROBE, **$11.**
A LADY OMEGA WATCH cost **$125.**
BRAUN HAIR DRYER, **$19.95.**
PUSH-BUTTON TAPE RECORDER, **$39.95.**
FIRE-RESISTANT ARTIFICIAL SIX-FOOT CHRISTMAS TREE, **$50.**
THE BOARD GAME CLUE cost **$8.95.**
STEREO 8-TRACK TAPE RECORDER, **$99.95.**
PING-PONG TABLE, **$24.95.**
BINOCULARS WITH CASE FEATURING TRANSISTOR AM/FM RADIO, **$40.**

REBUILT AND RELOCATED, THE LONDON BRIDGE WAS OPENED IN ARIZONA'S LAKE HAVASU CITY—IN THE MIDDLE OF THE DESERT.

The $70 million **JOHN F. KENNEDY CENTER** for the Performing Arts opened on September 8 in Washington, DC. The first piece performed was Leonard Bernstein's *Mass*, which Jacqueline Kennedy Onassis had asked the composer to write in memory of JFK.

cultural
milestones

LOOK MAGAZINE ANNOUNCED THAT IT WAS FOLDING AFTER 34 YEARS. MANAGEMENT BLAMED THE DECISION ON RISING POSTAL COSTS AND COMPETITION FROM TELEVISION.

A federal survey revealed that 31 percent of American college students had tried marijuana, and 14 percent confessed to being "regular smokers."

top-rated tv shows of the 1971 season:

1. "Marcus Welby, M.D." (ABC)

2. "The Flip Wilson Show" (NBC)

3. "Here's Lucy" (CBS)

4. "Ironside" (NBC)

5. "Gunsmoke" (CBS)

6. "The ABC Movie of the Week" (ABC)

7. "Hawaii Five-O" (CBS)

8. "Medical Center" (CBS)

9. "Bonanza" (NBC)

10. "The F.B.I." (ABC)

milestones

On March 4, Canadian Prime Minister **PIERRE TRUDEAU** married **MARGARET SINCLAIR,** 22, in a Roman Catholic ceremony in British Columbia. Prior to his nuptials, the 51-year-old bachelor had dated **BARBRA STREISAND.**

TRICIA NIXON, DAUGHTER OF PRESIDENT **RICHARD NIXON,** WED **EDWARD FINCH COX** ON JUNE 12.

D E A T H S

Coco Chanel,
grande dame of fashion, died on January 10 in Paris.

J. C. Penney,
founder of the department store that bore his name, died on February 12. He was 95.

François "Papa Doc" Duvalier,
president-for-life of Haiti, died on April 22 at 61.

Jim Morrison,
founder and lead singer of The Doors, died of a drug overdose in Paris on July 3.

Louis Armstrong,
jazz trumpet virtuoso, died on July 6 at 71.

Margaret Bourke-White,
pioneer photojournalist, died in Connecticut on August 27.

Nikita Khrushchev,
deposed leader of the Soviet Communist Party, died in obscurity in Moscow on September 11.

Duane Allman,
rock guitarist and founder of the Allman Brothers Band, 24, died on October 29.

David Sarnoff,
former head of RCA and founder of the National Broadcasting Company, died in New York on December 12.

births

EMMANUEL LEWIS, diminutive star of TV's "Webster," was born March 9 in New York City.

TIFFANY, bubble gum rock singer, was born in Norwalk, CA, on October 2.

WINONA RYDER, actress, born on October 29, was named after her hometown, Winona, Minnesota.

The Doors

1. **joy to the world** Three Dog Night
2. **maggie may** Rod Stewart
3. **it's too late** Carole King
4. **one bad apple** The Osmonds
5. **how can you mend a broken heart** The Bee Gees
6. **knock three times** Dawn
7. **brand new key** Melanie
8. **go away, little girl** Donny Osmond
9. **family affair** Sly & The Family Stone
10. **gypsys, tramps & thieves** Cher

hit music

Three Dog Night

Led Zeppelin

With release of their second album, **Stairway to Heaven,** polls showed that **Led Zeppelin,** the British rock trio featuring vocalist Robert Plant and ex-Yardbirds guitarist Jimmy Page, had surpassed the Beatles in popularity.

bestselling

fiction

1. **qb vii**
   leon uris

2. **love story**
   erich segal

3. **islands in the stream**
   ernest hemingway

4. **rich man, poor man**
   irwin shaw

5. **the new centurions**
   joseph wambaugh

6. **the crystal cave**
   mary stewart

7. **the exorcist**
   william peter blatty

8. **passenger to frankfurt**
   agatha christie

9. **the other**
   thomas tryon

10. **the bell jar**
    sylvia plath

books

15

IN BOXING, there was good news and bad news for Muhammad Ali. Four years after he was convicted of refusing army induction and stripped of his heavyweight title, Ali was cleared by the Supreme Court in an 8–0 vote. The bad news: Joe Frazier handed him his first loss in 31 professional bouts and won the world heavyweight boxing championship.

IN BASEBALL, HANK AARON JOINED BABE RUTH AND WILLIE MAYS TO BECOME THE THIRD PLAYER IN THE HISTORY OF THE GAME TO HIT 600 HOME RUNS.

vice president spiro agnew managed to steal the spotlight away from Arnold Palmer and other top pros at the Bob Hope Classic. He hit 3 spectators with his first 2 shots, then dropped his driver and drove his golf cart off in disgust. The White House had no comment.

Tennis star Billie Jean King became the first woman athlete to win $100,000 in one year.

IN AUTO RACING, THE UNSER NAME CONTINUED TO REIGN SUPREME. AL UNSER WON HIS 2ND INDY 500 IN A ROW, ADDING TO BROTHER BILLY'S 1968 VICTORY.

In golf, **LAURA BAUGH** won the U.S. Women's Amateur Golf championship in Atlanta. At 16, she was the youngest woman to hold the title.

sports

In football, Baltimore won its first Super Bowl ever by defeating Dallas 16–13 with a field goal by rookie Jim O'Brien in the last 10 seconds.

ping-pong

became all the rage after an American team visited China to play Peking. The Ping-Pongers were the first group of U.S. citizens to visit the Communist stronghold in 20 years.

top 5 box-office champs and earnings

1. *Fiddler on the Roof* (United Artists) — $38,251,000

2. *Billy Jack* (Warner Bros.) — $32,500,000

3. *The French Connection* (20th Century-Fox) — $26,315,000

4. *The Summer of '42* (Warner Bros.) — $20,500,000

5. *Diamonds Are Forever* (United Artists) — $19,726,829

FOREIGN FILMS FOUND A NEW VOGUE WITH AMERICAN AUDIENCES. FAVORITES INCLUDED PASOLINI'S *THE DECAMERON,* DE SICA'S *THE GARDEN OF THE FINZI-CONTINIS,* VISCONTI'S *DEATH IN VENICE,* BERTOLUCCI'S *THE CONFORMIST,* AND ROHMER'S *CLAIRE'S KNEE.*

Oscar winners for 1971 movies: ***The French Connection*** took Best Picture, Best Director (**William Friedkin**), and Best Actor (**Gene Hackman**). The ***Last Picture Show*** boasted awards for Best Supporting Actor (**Ben Johnson**) and Best Supporting Actress (**Cloris Leachman**). Best Actress was **Jane Fonda** in ***Klute.***

movies

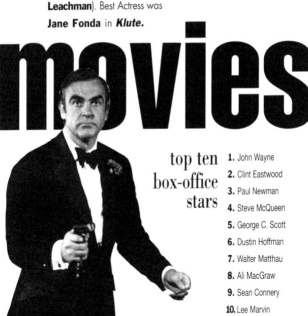

top ten
box-office
stars

1. John Wayne
2. Clint Eastwood
3. Paul Newman
4. Steve McQueen
5. George C. Scott
6. Dustin Hoffman
7. Walter Matthau
8. Ali MacGraw
9. Sean Connery
10. Lee Marvin

'71

Sales of small imports (Volkswagen, Toyota and Datsun) skyrocketed, while Detroit saw purchases of traditional luxury cars decline precipitously. "Economical, everyday transportation" became the watchword of the auto industry. The

It was the year of the Incredible Shrinking Car.

cars

twin specters of inflation and recession spurred consumers to opt for the practical over the plush. New concerns over the state of the environment and air pollution contributed to the trend toward smaller, less wasteful vehicles. Two compacts, the Dodge Dart and the Plymouth Valiant, marked the American auto industry's entry into the econo-car market.

The Super Beetle.

On February 10, Alexander's, a New York department store, hosted its first-ever hotpants show, and women everywhere were squeezing into the shorter-than-short shorts. Hotpants could be in anything from sleek leather to glis-

"Hotpants fever" swept the fashion world this year.

fashion

tening satin, or sprinkled with rhinestones for evening wear. The uniform of the year became hotpants half concealed under a shaggy midi-length fur coat that covered the tops of knee-high leather boots.

All kinds of furs were accepted and expected in 1971. Capes, coats, and jackets made from a multitude of pelts—including monkey—were huge. A fad for forties styles betrayed nostalgia for a simpler, happier time.

During the day, white was a big color. Women could be seen wearing sharp white shorts, pants, shirts, and short dresses. This was highlighted by streaks of black or flounces of pink taffeta, chiffon or crepe. At dinner, chiffon, prints and long shirts were all the rage.

Pantsuits were everywhere, as women began adding trousers to their roster of appropriate officewear.

final factoid

For the twelfth straight year, Fifi reigned supreme. Poodles continued to represent the #1 breed of purebred dog registered in the country.

credits

archive photos: inside front cover, pages 1, 7, 10, 13, 15, 17, 20, 22, 23, 25, inside back cover.

associated press: pages 2, 3, 4, 6, 7, 16.

photofest: pages 9, 11, 12, 18, 19.

photo research:
alice albert

coordination:
rustyn birch

design:
carol bokuniewicz design
mutsumi hyuga

'71